W9-ANZ-357

EXPLORING THE WORLD OF

Bees

Tracy C. Read

FIREFLY BOOKS

A FIREFLY BOOK

Published by Firefly Books Ltd. 2011

First Printing

Publisher Cataloging-in-Publication Data (U.S.)
Read, Tracy C.
  Exploring the world of bees / Tracy C. Read.
  [ ] p. : col. photos. ; cm.
Includes index.
Summary: The beauty, significance and habits of bees.
ISBN-13: 978-1-55407-882-0 (bound)
ISBN-10: 1-55407-882-2 (bound)
ISBN-13: 978-1-55407-955-1 (pbk.)
ISBN-10: 1-55407-955-1 (pbk.)
1. Bees. I. Title.
595.79 dc22   QL563.R434 2011

Library and Archives Canada
  Cataloguing in Publication
Read, Tracy C.
  Exploring the world of bees /
  Tracy C. Read.
Includes index.
ISBN-13: 978-1-55407-882-0 (bound)
ISBN-10: 1-55407-882-2 (bound)
ISBN-13: 978-1-55407-955-1 (pbk.)
ISBN-10: 1-55407-955-1 (pbk.)
1. Bees--Juvenile literature. I. Title.
QL563.R43 2011
j595.79'9   C2011-902337-7

Published in the United States by
Firefly Books (U.S.) Inc.
P.O. Box 1338, Ellicott Station
Buffalo, New York 14205

Published in Canada by
Firefly Books Ltd.
66 Leek Crescent
Richmond Hill, Ontario L4B 1H1

The Publisher gratefully acknowledges the financial support for our publishing program by the Government of Canada through the Canada Book Fund as administered by the Department of Canadian Heritage.

Cover and interior design by
Janice McLean/Bookmakers Press Inc.

Printed in Canada

CONTENTS

BENIGN BEES
Unlike most wasps, which feed their larvae insect prey, nearly all bees are herbivores, raising their young on plant pollen and nectar.

MEET THE BEES

After a long, cool, mostly rainy spring, the bees at last appeared in our garden. One sunny morning, I watched as a bumblebee landed on a tiny purple flower and began to sip the nectar inside the blossom. Its sheer bulk caused the stem to swing down like an unbalanced teeter-totter, but the bee hung on, finishing its sweet drink before flying off, its furry body and legs dusted with yellow pollen.

Scientists have identified more than 20,000 bee species in the world, and close to 4,000 species are found in North America. (Some, like the honeybee, aren't native to this continent but were imported by European settlers.) Most of us are familiar with the highly social honeybees and bumblebees that live in busy colonies. Yet the majority of bees are, in fact, solitary bees that live on their own or in loose associations with neighbors, burrowing into the ground or into plant stems or old wood to make their nests.

As the bumblebee in our spring garden transferred pollen to the next flower, it was playing its part in pollination, a process that insects and plants have shared for more than 100 million years. By enabling the cross-fertilization that produces the next generation of plants, pollination makes our lives possible too. Let's learn more about bees, whose day jobs in our backyards have such far-reaching consequences for the planet.

ANATOMY LESSON

With so many thousands of bee species in the world, it's not surprising to discover that these flying insects display a dazzling array of body shapes, sizes and colors and a range of distinguishing adaptations.

Generally speaking, however, the bee comes in a fairly standard package, one that is designed for flight, food detection and the efficient transport of a daily cargo of nectar and pollen.

The bee's soft body is covered by a protective exoskeleton made of a hard material called chitin and is divided into three parts: the head; the thorax, to which its two sets of wings and three sets of legs are attached; and the abdomen, which contains the digestive and reproductive organs.

Three simple eyes on the bee's forehead detect changes in light intensity, while large compound eyes on either side of its head gather information about distance, color and flickering light. Two antennae also help the bee zero in on flowering plants.

The bee's mouthparts are composed of upper and lower jaws and a long, hairy tongue that the bee uses to extract nectar from flowers.

As the bee moves about on all six legs, it is aided by clawlike tarsi on each leg. The legs are also used when collecting and transferring pollen and for grooming.

FLIGHT CONTROL

A bee's wings, attached to its thorax, are animated by flight muscles. By fanning its wings, a bee can cool the nest, and by vibrating the muscles, it is able to generate heat.

TAKES A LICKING

As a bee unfurls its tongue to sip
nectar from a flower, powdery pollen
sticks to the hairs on its body and legs.
Dense brushes of hair on the hind legs
of female bees are used to transport
pollen back to the nest. In honeybees
and bumblebees, these structures
are more developed and are
known as pollen baskets.

With over 20,000 species worldwide, telling one bee from another is a job for an expert. In any given species, there are physical differences between males and females and also between bees that perform separate tasks. The honeybee, below, with its striped abdomen, and the furry bumblebee, far right, are easier to identify.

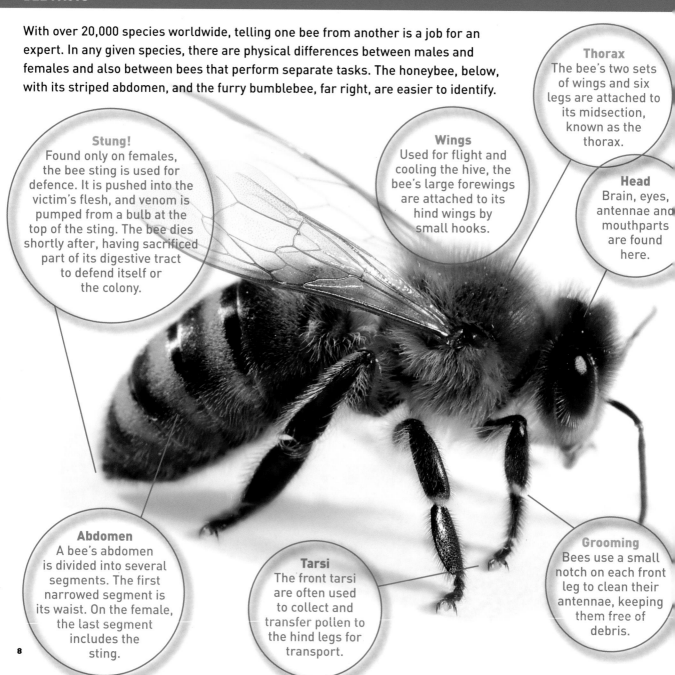

Thorax
The bee's two sets of wings and six legs are attached to its midsection, known as the thorax.

Stung!
Found only on females, the bee sting is used for defence. It is pushed into the victim's flesh, and venom is pumped from a bulb at the top of the sting. The bee dies shortly after, having sacrificed part of its digestive tract to defend itself or the colony.

Wings
Used for flight and cooling the hive, the bee's large forewings are attached to its hind wings by small hooks.

Head
Brain, eyes, antennae and mouthparts are found here.

Abdomen
A bee's abdomen is divided into several segments. The first narrowed segment is its waist. On the female, the last segment includes the sting.

Tarsi
The front tarsi are often used to collect and transfer pollen to the hind legs for transport.

Grooming
Bees use a small notch on each front leg to clean their antennae, keeping them free of debris.

Antennae
Covered with thick hairs, two segmented antennae aid the bee in identifying textures, temperature, odor and taste.

Compound eyes
The bee's two compound eyes contain thousands of tiny eyes that individually receive and communicate information about color, movement and intensity of light.

Simple eyes
Called ocelli, three simple eyes on top of the bee's head monitor changing light conditions and help the bee calculate the approach of darkness.

Tongue
The bee's tongue, or proboscis, is long and hairy, the better to absorb nectar as it drinks.

CRUNCH THOSE ABS
On a frosty morning, an Arctic bumblebee must raise its body temperature before it can take flight. Sitting in a resting position, it contracts its flight muscles until all systems are go.

Forelegs, middle legs and hind legs
All six of the bee's legs are covered with hairs that serve as combs and brushes to pick up pollen as the bee moves from one flowering plant to the next.

AIR MILES ANYONE?

Flight is an expensive mode of travel — a bee burns up 50 times as much energy in the air as it spends on the ground. Still, for a flower-hopping pollinator, it's the only way to go.

NATURAL TALENTS

Picture yourself as a bee. Your assignment? To go out on daily missions through hostile territory and retrieve the substances necessary for life. You're tiny. And you're vulnerable to predators, including birds and mammals and even other flying insects, like your cousin, the wasp. You have one defensive weapon, but if you use it, you'll die. How do you make it home alive?

Fortunately, the bee is beautifully designed for the challenge. Its ability to fly is key, but flying to and from specific destinations demands other skills. The bee's brain contains hundreds of thousands of neurons that communicate with one another and perform separate complex tasks. It also houses a nervous system that sends and receives messages to and from other parts of the bee's body.

While the human eye sees a crisp, focused image, the bee's two large compound eyes collect thousands of bits of light that appear as a fuzzy mosaic of dots of different intensities. As it flies, the bee is able to interpret the broken patterns and outlines of vegetation and the forms and contours of different flowers, even from a range of angles and heights. It can also identify simple shapes, such as the round opening to its nest.

The bee sees colors as well, though its eyes are far more sensitive to ultraviolet than to red.

TONGUE LASHING

A bee's long tongue, top, is extended to suck up liquids. When not in use, it is tucked under the bee's "chin." Above, a bumblebee maneuvers its way into the flower of a wild columbine.

GOURD GOURMET

Some bees are pollination specialists. This squash bee, for example, has developed a special taste for the flowers of squash, zucchinis and pumpkins. Pollen is carried back to the nest on the dense thatch of hair on its hind legs. Although it is a solitary bee, it may dig its ground nest close to the nests of other bees.

As with humans, the bee's senses of smell and taste are closely connected, and its two segmented antennae pick up signals about both. The antennae transmit information about a flower's scent and its location, and they are handy for "sniffing" a flower close up and detecting sweetness. (The bee's legs are also able to detect sweetness.) Scientists speculate that antennae may be able to measure temperature and humidity levels too.

The bee's mouthparts are organs of touch *and* taste. Jaws are used as biting and chewing tools when the bee makes its nest or is forced to slice open a flower to reach the nectar. The tongue sucks up nectar, honey and water and is also used by ground-nesting bees to tidy up nest cells.

In fact, the entire bee is built for receptivity, thanks to sensitive hairs all over its body that supply clues to everything from gravity and the position of its legs to how to manage wind flow and direction as it flies.

EASY BEING GREEN
Attracted to the taste of salt in human perspiration, this metallic-green bee is a sweat bee. A member of the Halictidae family, it feeds on pollen and typically makes its home in the ground.

SIGHT
While the bee can detect light, color and movement and can see in almost every direction, its vision is fuzzy.

HEARING
Although bees do not have ears, they can "hear" vibrations through their lower legs.

SMELL
Two antennae, moving independently, can "sniff out" and pinpoint odors in the bee's vicinity.

TASTE
bee is all about e, which it experi- s not only with its gue but with its antennae and legs too.

TOUCH
From the tip of its antennae to its hairy body and legs, the hypersensitive bee is wired for touch.

13

BEE LIFESTYLES

Bees that live cooperatively in a large colony are described as social bees. Those that don't are considered solitary bees, because the female lays her eggs in a single-family nest. Depending on the circumstances, however, the so-called solitary bees often live in situations that fall somewhere between these two extremes.

Its genius for working well with others has made the honeybee one of the planet's most famous social bees. That remarkable team spirit is showcased in its honeycomb, a stunning piece of animal architecture that shelters thousands of bees, all working together to rear young bees and produce honey.

The honeycomb itself is constructed of six-sided cells precisely engineered by worker bees using wax extruded from a gland on the abdomen. In the lower part of the hive, the cells serve as nurseries for the bee's early life stages, from egg, larva and cocoon to young adult. In the upper part of the hive, the cells are stocked with honey.

Honeybee society is based on a disciplined, age-related division of labor among female residents. Cell cleaning, larvae care, food provision for the queen (whose sole job is to lay eggs), new cell construction, foraging for nectar and pollen and

BEE ALL THAT YOU CAN BE

The solitary carpenter bee, top, chews its way into old wood to make a home, while the honeybee, center, lives in a waxen honeycomb community. Often mistaken for a bumblebee, the solitary mining bee, bottom, prefers to excavate a nest in hard clay.

A REAL CUTUP

Using its mouth to cut away pieces of leaves to line its nest has earned this bee the name leafcutter. A woodland native, this solitary bee nests in an existing wood cavity or a hollow plant stem. It is considered a very efficient wild pollinator.

unloading and storing the returning food supplies are all on the daily list of the worker bees' chores.

If you're a male honeybee, or drone, your job is to venture out to rendezvous with a virgin queen, a meeting that ends, rather dramatically, in your death. Drones that are unsuccessful in their quest to mate return to the hive.

The familiar bumblebee is also a social bee, though on a much more modest scale. Unlike honeybees, which survive the winter by clustering in the hive and generating life-sustaining heat, the bumblebee colony usually dies out at the end of the summer, after the late-season males have mated with a queen. The surviving queens hibernate in the soil until spring.

When the days get warmer, the queen emerges from hibernation, grabs a quick snack of nectar for energy and a supply of pollen and flies off to scout out a location for her nest. A suitable site might be a thatch of dead grass or the abandoned nest of a bird or mouse in a hollow on the ground. Inside, the

THE GREAT DIVIDE

When a honeybee colony grows too big to sustain itself, the queen and a share of the workers swarm off to set up another hive, leaving a new queen behind to carry on.

queen builds a round, nectar-filled wax cup to serve as a food source and skillfully shapes a ball of pollen into which she lays a cluster of eggs. These will become the next generation of bumblebee daughters that will forage for food for the colony and become care-givers to successive batches of new bees. As their numbers grow, the nest is expanded. Bumblebee colonies typically contain between 30 and 400 members.

Many of North America's solitary bees, including the mining bees, the plasterer bees and the

I WANT TO BEE ALONE

As it collects nectar, the short-tongued solitary plasterer bee transfers pollen from flower to flower. This bee makes its home in a hole in the ground or in a rock crevice, lining its nest with a waterproofing secretion.

squash bees, establish their homes underground, digging narrow tunnels that lead to special chambers called brood cells. Each brood cell is stocked with a single egg and enough food (a mixture of nectar and protein-rich pollen) to sustain the new bee into adulthood, since the female usually dies before the young emerge. Many ground nesters locate their homes close to other bee families, in a behavior that is described as "gregarious."

Carpenter bees prefer to chew into aged or rotten wood to set up nests but often do so alongside other bees in an old log or a ramshackle building. Still others, like the mason bees and leafcutters, may construct their nests in plant stems or tree twigs.

Typically, a bee's life is a one-season wonder. Only a hibernating female lives until the next season.

SOCIAL BEE STUDIES

Humans have been fascinated by the social life of bees for thousands of years. Perhaps that's because we can't help being intrigued by another animal's success at living so productively (and, for the most part, so peaceably) in a complex, cooperative society.

Honeybee society is organized around the queen, and she is essential to the future of the colony through her ability to lay about half a million eggs over the course of her roughly two years of life. Her daughters, the worker bees, feed her and make sure she's clean and healthy, because they are all committed to the greater good of the colony.

As the worker bees move through their much shorter lives, they bring incredible dedication to the business of the hive, whether it's heating and cooling it, checking on the larvae-occupied cells, which they might do as many as 2,000 times in a week, cleaning and renovating old cells or simply tirelessly patrolling their home to see what needs to be done next — and then doing it. People should be so dependable.

Especially impressive is the foraging bee's ability, upon returning to the hive, to communicate to its waiting sisters the exact location and distance of a rich store of flower nectar. This it does by performing its famous "waggle dance," a wireless code delivered by a vibrating bee that is as accurate as any global positioning system.

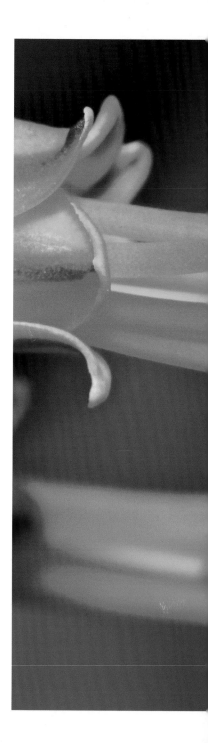

PLAN BEE

As the summer draws to a close, fewer flowers are in bloom and the supply of nectar in the honeycomb begins to decline. To preserve limited resources, the workers may start to physically expel the drones from the hive. Having failed to mate with a queen, the males no longer serve a purpose.

THE GOLDEN TICKET

Sex helps make the world go round, and that's just as true for plants as it is for animals. But without flying pollinators like bees to fertilize plants by transferring tiny grains of pollen from the male anthers of one flower to the female stigma of another, much of the fruit and seed production that ensures the next generation simply would not take place.

To understand how important bees are in our lives, think about what you eat every day. A huge portion of our food (one out of every three bites) depends on bees, including most fruits and vegetables and crops such as alfalfa and clover, which in turn provide food for the cows that give us milk. Your cotton t-shirt and jeans got their start with the help of bees too.

In the steamy tropical rainforests, the pollinating duties of bees contribute to one of the Earth's richest ecosystems, while in temperate regions, bushes and flowering plants rely on their visits. And in dry desert climates, the bees' intervention may be what stands between a barren, wind - swept landscape and the production of food and livable habitat for wildlife.

Just something to think about the next time you see one of these hardworking little flying insects buzz past.

WHAT'S ON THE MENU?

The food on your plate didn't begin life in a supermarket. Bees play a part in every meal we eat, from breakfast fruit, such as peaches, watermelon and cherries, to snack foods, like sunflower seeds, and vegetables, such as squash and zucchini. Even the mustard on your hotdog is made possible by the attentions of a passing bee.

A BUG'S LIFE

While wind disperses many plant seeds, as do birds and mammals, flying insects like this domesticated honeybee are key to guaranteeing the next harvest of a wide variety of food crops. The role of native bees is even more critical.

21

SWEET SORROW

The once gentle hobby of beekeeping might today be unrecognizable to the 17th-century European colonists who first brought their hives to North America. Alongside the settlers, the honeybees prospered, carrying on their duties of pollination and providing honey, improving the taste and productivity of crops and doing a little colonizing of the New World themselves.

A few centuries later, beekeeping has become big business. Stackable hives are loaded onto flatbed trucks and driven around the country, and hundreds of thousands of honeybees-for-hire work the blossoms of single crops, like almonds and grapes, before being returned home.

But big business can be stressful, and the bees appear to be paying the price. In 2006, beekeepers began to report missing honeybees. Bees had suffered from diseases and pests before, but in what came to be called Colony Collapse Disorder, large numbers of honeybees were simply failing to return to their hives.

Scientists and beekeepers have been working frantically to solve the mystery. Is the culprit toxic pesticides, mites, viruses, bacteria, immune deficiency, stress, climate change or some combination of some or all of these? Nobody seems to agree. What we do know is that the critical business of pollination has changed in ways that humans can no longer control.

HAVE BEES, WILL TRAVEL

With the human population growing worldwide, there is an increasing demand for food. But if honeybee colonies are collapsing, can native bees take over the essential job of these portable pollinators?